# To Achieve It...
# You Must First Believe It!

# To Believe It...
# You Must First Dream It!

J. Brian Bergeron

# Dream It

To Believe It...You Must First Dream It!

Dedicated to my

two beautiful daughters,

Alexa Katherine & Abby Frances.

May God bless you

with the courage to pursue

your wildest dreams.

Dream It

As far back as I can remember, dreaming has been an inspirational part of my life. Whether as a young boy in the backyard shooting basketball and dreaming I was "Pistol Pete" Maravich, or now, as a young man working to turn my dreams into reality, my dreams have always been a motivating and driving force in my life. In my 41 years I have learned that few great things happen by chance. Almost all great feats begin with a dream and are realized by the endless pursuit of those dreams.

It is my hope that all who read this will challenge themselves to believe in the power of their dreams. More importantly, I hope the parents who read this will encourage and lead their children in the pursuit of their dreams.

*Dream It*

I am eternally grateful to my parents, Ralph and Elenita Bergeron, for supporting this "Dreamer." Also, I am thankful that I married a woman like Jill. No matter how ridiculous some of my ideas might sound, she has always been supportive. I would be remiss if I didn't thank my long time assistant and friend, Sherry. Thanks for always walking by my side in the pursuit of "our" dreams.

The quotations in this book are thoughts that I have written over the years. It is my wish that this little book is an enlightening experience to all who read it.

Enthusiastically yours,

Nothing is impossible
to him who dreams.

*Dream It*

Don't always dream of
becoming great.

Dream of helping others
become great.

*Dream It*

Trust in your dreams—

not in your fears.

Dream It

The only way to make a dream unique is to put yourself in it.

*Dream It*

A young man's dreams
show his maturity.

An older man's dreams
express his youth.

Dream It

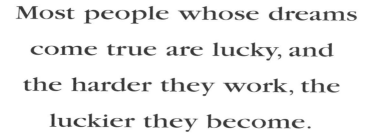

Most people whose dreams
come true are lucky, and
the harder they work, the
luckier they become.

*Dream It*

12

I often dream about God
and wonder if he really
looks like George Burns.

*Dream It*

All work and no dreams

makes for a dull man.

*Dream It*

If your dream doesn't include God, hopefully it won't come true.

Dream *It*

Surround yourself with people who are pursuing their dreams instead of those who have already fulfilled them.

It will be more fun.

*Dream It*

If Columbus had no dreams,

he'd still be sitting on shore.

Dream It

A true friend would rather
see your dreams come
true instead of his own.

*Dream It*

If all your dreams
come true, your dreams
are too small.

Dream It

# To achieve it...

## you must first believe it!

# To believe it...

## you must first dream it!

*Dream It*

I often dream of being

the yeast that makes

the dough rise.

Dream It

If you can't start a fire
without a spark,
then you can't start a dream
without an imagination.

*Dream It*

When I was younger, I dreamed
of making my parents proud.

Now, I dream of making
my children proud.

Dream It

Keep God in your dreams,

and He will keep you in His.

Dream It

Many a man's dreams were
ahead of their time.

*Dream It*

You'll only go as far as
your dreams take you.

Dream It

26

Always include others

in your dreams.

It will be much

more rewarding.

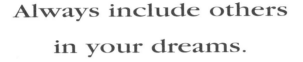

Dream It

I often pray that when I stop
dreaming—I stop breathing.

*Dream It*

Every young basketball player
dreams of being Michael Jordan.

So does Michael Jordan.

Dream It

Give a dreamer a chance.
There is nothing more
gratifying than contributing
to someone else's dreams.

Dream It

Every prisoner dreams
of being free.

I'm glad I don't have
to dream about that.

Dream It

What was a dream yesterday
may be reality today.

What is reality today may be
a dream tomorrow.

*Dream It*

On the seventh day

God rested—and dreamed.

*Dream It*

Take a long walk in the
rain and dream.
When the sun comes out,
it will be your sign to
pursue that dream.

*Dream It*

I often dream of being as intelligent as my dad. Just when I think I am, he teaches me something new.

Dream It

One of your dreams

should be that your children's

dreams are realized.

*Dream It*

Behind every great man
there lies a great woman
and a great dream.

*Dream It*

Don't dream about living life
instead of fighting it . . .do it!

Dream It

Self-righteous people call
themselves visionaries.

Humble people call
themselves dreamers.

*Dream It*

If dreaming were a drug,

I'd be an addict.

*Dream It*

Dream until your

dreams come true.

Then dream some more.

*Dream It*

God has a dream for me.
With His help I can make
that dream come true.

Dream It

I often dream of becoming

a great storyteller.


Kids love great storytellers.


*Dream It*

It is better to dream and your
dream not be realized than to
not have dreamed at all.

Dream It

Some people dream of
becoming a pilot. I dream
of owning the airline.

Dream It

Many times I've dreamed of
never owing the IRS money.
This is the only dream
I've given up on.

*Dream It*

Show me a dreamer, and
I'll show you a leader.

Show me a person with
no dreams, and I'll find a
dreamer he can follow.

Dream It

Dream about Heaven while eating breakfast, and your day will start on a perfect note.

Dream *It*

Do everything you can now to make your dreams come true because when you die, you're dead for a long time.

*Dream It*

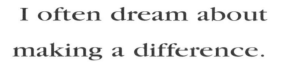

I often dream about
making a difference.

When all is said and
done, I hope this dream
will have come true.

*Dream It*

All great things start

with a dream.


Just ask God.

Dream It

Life without dreams is like
bread without butter.

No matter how you slice it,
it's just not as good.

Dream It

Try sharing your dreams

instead of your problems.

You will make more friends.

*Dream It*

Winners are driven
by their dreams.

Losers are strangled
by their nightmares.

*Dream It*

Always believe in the
power of your dreams.

Dream It

Be generous in your
dreams, and it will carry
over into your life.

Dream It

Dream enthusiastically.

Dream It

I often dream of seeing my
grandmother again.

When I do, I'll know I'm
in Heaven.

*Dream It*

Make one of your dreams
to help someone else fulfill
one of their dreams.

*Dream It*

Many of us dream of finding God, but how many of us actually look for Him?

*Dream It*

Act upon your dreams.
A dream without action is
like a new car without gas.
It's nice, but it can't take
you where you want to go.

Dream It

Everyone has dreams.
The difference between
those whose dreams come
true and those that don't is
the dreamer himself.

*Dream It*

Everyone knows you
can't steal second base with one
foot on first. But what we
all must realize is that you can't
get to first without,
at some point, having dreamed
of playing the game.

Dream It

I often dream of what my
funeral will be like.

I hope some people show up.

*Dream It*

When you're driving

to work – dream.

When you're mowing

the lawn – dream.

When you're jogging – dream.

But when you're playing with

your children – play.

*Dream It*

Dreaming is contagious.

So is complacency.

The choice is yours.

*Dream It*

A man who does not pursue

his dreams is like a wild animal

that does not pursue his prey.

They both will starve.

*Dream It*

Dream.

Encourage your spouse to dream.

Encourage your kids to dream.

A family that dreams together,

grows together.

*Dream It*

The greatest dream of all is to one day see the face of God.

Dream It

When you present an idea
and someone says, "You're
dreaming," say, "Thank you."

*Dream It*

My mom died in June of 2000.
I often dream of Mom and Dad
being together again. I know
Dad has the same dream.

Dream It

If someone laughs at one of
your dreams, share another
dream with him.

*Dream It*

Pursue your dreams today,

because in two days tomorrow

will be yesterday.

Dream It

Everyone dreams of being
successful, but how many of us
are willing to pay the price?

*Dream It*

God loves dreamers, as long
as He is the central focus.

Dream It

# Dream Big!!!

Dream It

Success is chasing your passion, dreaming big dreams, growing old but never becoming old, and, along the way, constantly striving to make a difference.

Dream *It*

For more information about

Dream It and it's products and services,

please contact:

## Dream It

Post Office Box 344

Tifton, Georgia 31793

1-888-4DREAM9

dream-it@friendlycity.net

## Dream It

78